THE PERSPECTIVE OF A RAINBOW

AARON WILLIAMS

REBEL NETWORK

First printing, 2020.
Editor: D'Shene Cotton
ISBN: 978-0-578-69587-7

Rebel Network
P.O 2556
Rialto, CA 92376

Dedication

To all the people who inspired these emotions, making me enhance my thought process.

Conversation Topics

THE PERSPECTIVE OF A RAINBOW

Introduction

Let's put this thing we call life into perspective and begin with the end in mind. Have you ever wondered how people will speak of you at your funeral? What would they say about your actions and the true content of your character? Through the years, I have learned not to hang myself on the opinions of others and boldly live outside of that small box they decided to place me in. I have no time nor desire to live a life "according" to others. This is what matters the most, right? A life well defined that exists outside of the judgement of people... Yet, I still find myself living and existing to serve others. Not because I am seeking approval or care what others may think of me, but it is because I genuinely care.

My middle name is Je'von. It was not until a couple weeks before I began writing this that I learned it meant "Gift from God." It's funny because I asked my parents why they chose that name and their only reasoning for choice was that it started with the letter "j". You see, God placed me on this planet with a purpose and I'm still figuring it out. I care about how I impact and influence those around me. My desire is to be that rare person that inspires, uplifts and contribute to the betterment of my community regardless of the cost. It is who I am. My life has not been perfect nor without fault. There were times in my life where I have shared beds, slept on tile floors, flimsy coffee tables, and even bed-bug infested couches. Yeah, you read that right. I literally had to make sure the bed bugs did not bite. I know your skin is crawling, but I promise there is a purpose for this story. During this time, I began to feel like a burden on the people around me. I despised this feeling greatly and this is what drove me to become more independent and more so pushed me into my anti-social tendencies. I set out to take on a journey of independence. I did not WANT help. I did not NEED help. I did not and do not want to converse nor hangout. I just wanted to find success and find it on my own terms.

The incomparable Nipsey Hussle once said, "I went through every emotion with trying to pursue what I'm doing..." Every emotion we encounter is inevitable. Our emotions can be raw, intense, subtle, passionate, and even uncontrollable based on a certain set of circumstances. Emotions can shape reality. They can be the driving force that propels to the next level or the greatest obstacle if unchecked. In my life, I have seen my fair share of trials and tribulations and I can say that the greatness of God got me through with his uncanny ability to show me that there must be a delicate balance between our emotions and our perspective in order to thrive.

That is what this book is about; perspective and emotion and how it shapes experiences. How we see things (perception) and how we feel (emotion) are the reasons why we think how we think, act how we act (react), and feel the way we feel. Think about the latest Snicker's commercial. Someone feeling high strung and stressed until they are given a Snickers bar and then we realize they were really a whole different person that was in their feelings because they were hungry. Get the point? Are you beginning to understand the relationship between the two and how they shape experiences?

It's like cause and effect. At any given time, one can influence the other. They work in a tandem. As great as they are individually, they are even more powerful together. Imagine Kobe Bryant and Michael Jordan in a two-man basketball tournament. They are both amazing individually, but what happens when they begin to work together? Of course, you would worry about two dominant powerhouses on the court at the same time and pray their alter egos do not take over. But you can also imagine if either one had the hot hand and witness how their energies can begin to feed off one another. Same concept with perspective and emotion.

Perspective and emotion are not only best friends, they are each other's day one homies...until they are not. They can be the worst of enemies if not managed properly and bring out some undesirable characteristics. They are like Sour Patch Kids, sour because you are in a foul mood and then sweet because you decided not to let your feelings determine the outcome. Again, how you perceive a situation can influence emotions and vice versa. This was a lesson that heavily, but slowly, impacted my lifestyle and determined how I began to conduct and convey myself. It took a long time to understand how these two were interrelated. Not because it was a hard concept to grasp, but because I did not evaluate situations and simply put the two together. I had to begin to ask myself the real question, how does one influence the other? To get to the root of these two co- stars, I had to understand their meaning.

What is perspective? It is how we view things, how we analyze and determine a course of action. It is our "particular attitude" towards things. When we perceive something in a certain manner, we then evoke a certain emotion. Each perspective easily carries its own emotion. It is about your frame of reference or that position in which you define experiences. We have heard the term from a "30,000-foot view." This encompasses the belief that seeing the whole picture from a distance influences interpretation. For instance, it is easier to discuss an abusive relationship from a macro level versus it being a personal experience. How close you are to a situation or your vantage point will determine the joy, heartache, happiness, heartbreak… the emotion you will feel.

A simple shift in perspective can easily shift emotion. What's crazy about this is that it does not have to necessarily be your own, it could be the perspective of someone else involved. One of my grandmother's favorite sayings was, "it is, what it is." I remember thinking that the words were not fluid. That they would never change and that our realities are solidified in concrete. But if we focused on our ability to manage our emotions based on our vantage point, we could effectively deduce a rational outcome. Be real. We as humans are not always rational, and it is ok. Why? Because we are human.

There are varying degrees of emotions and from what I experienced; every day was a different one. Nothing has been more fulfilling than experiencing a rainbow of emotion. The colors on the rainbow represent more than simply what they are. Do you remember the nursery rhyme used to help us remember our colors? Red, orange, yellow, green, blue, purple…These colors represent the most common emotions amongst people, thus being referred to as "The Rainbow of Emotion". For instance, red represents love or anger, yellow for happiness, or blue for sadness. Each color represents a set of different emotions and are generally agreed upon; however, there may be some differences. It is all based on your perspective. I'll share with you the emotions I most identified with the based on my experiences.

I have been constantly told that I have an old soul. The past two years have allowed me to grow and mature beyond my years. It has not only allowed me to better understand myself, but other people as well. It is important to understand others to consider and examine their intentions and perspectives in a situation. It pushed my mental barriers farther than I ever knew they could go. All because I understood the intriguing relationship between two everyday concepts.

I am self-reliant; I rarely went to others for anything. When sifting through perspectives and emotions, a lot of conversations took place between me, myself, and I. This was not just due to the quarantine, but it was plenty of days where I continuously talked, but never spoke aloud. Take this journey through my thought process. While reading, don't think of this as a book, but envision a conversation. Envision you and I sitting in front of a cozy fire, with a caramel macchiato or glass of Cabernet Sauvignon talking about our experiences. This is simply a conversation between you, I, and our thoughts.

Red: The Color of Love, Anger, & Passion

Red is probably the most identifiable color on the rainbow. When you see this color, you automatically connect with one of these three emotions almost immediately. Red is such an intense color that washes over you completely allowing you to bathe in its warmth. It is one of the only colors that represents conflicting emotions, such as love and anger. These are the most powerful of emotions and if unchecked, can be dangerous.

There was a period in my life where I allowed the power of emotions to take me over by storm. I wanted the feeling of love. I made myself vulnerable with a person I was "in like" with just to get a taste of this raw emotion. For the first time in a long time, I began to willingly open up my heart and mind. I was in love with the feeling of having this massive weight of being constantly on guard disappear. This is where the dichotomy exists in the rainbow. Love. Anger.

Remember, I am vulnerable at this point, so when this person that I was "in like" with did something that violated my expectations, I found myself in a state of confusion. I didn't look at it from a different perspective or from anyone else's point of view. All I knew was how I felt, and it allowed irrational anger and passion to obstruct my view. At that juncture, I knew nothing would change if I remained the same. So, I worked hard on my emotional intelligence to protect the peace in my life and keep myself in check.

LOVE

This is not me being in my feelings, but I was in love with love. At one point, I craved it. I felt it was needed to help improve my mental status and my overall view of life. LL Cool J and my vantage point said I needed love, right? Well, according to Maslow's Hierarchy of Needs, after basic needs such as food and safety, the next is love and belonging. Imagine that…Whether if it's friendship, intimacy, or family, we need a sense of connection. Maslow highlights that it is not just about feeling loved but showing love as well. So, the next time you are alone in your room, staring at the wall and then the back of your mind, you hear your conscious call. Telling you need a girl that's as sweet as dove, for the first time in my life, I see I need love. Shout out Uncle L! Point is, we all need love.

Although, I naturally gravitated towards exemplifying love towards others, that was not always my end game. I was more focused on receiving it rather than giving it. There are times where I showed so much love so I can simply get it back. Everything goes back to intent. Why we do the things we do. If we are only loving others to get love in return, our perspective becomes skewed and it is easier to violate expectations, setting us up for failure. I now give love and simply put that positive energy in air with the idea that it would become contagious.

My main sense of love was emotional intimacy. Emotional intimacy involves the relationship between people which allows the secure sharing of feelings that are accompanied by affirmation and understanding. There is a saying that says a person must give both their "head and heart." Your head holds your agenda. It is what you plan to accomplish. Your heart, on the other hand, is the reason why and how you feel about it. Transparency is key to emotional intimacy allowing people to develop relationships more naturally.

My grandmother used to say, "Don't tell everybody everything. Keep some things to yourself." Yet, self-disclosure is vital to deepening connections. We as people are different, but finding a common ground is crucial to getting to next level. Our comfort levels in expressing this kind of intimacy can feel uncomfortable and cause one to become hesitant, especially when it is not reciprocated. There was a time where I felt I had to have both a sense of affirmation and understanding with a person before my comfort level rose. However, when you feel like emotional intimacy is something you need, even the slightest expression of it places you in a vulnerable position. You are willing to be something to a person who is not willing to be that for you.

As a person of compassion your love is unmatched. You give off a tremendous amount of quality energy and you expect that back. This is an investment. When you invest into anything, you set a marker to represent the minimum satisfactory return on investment. For example, you are giving $100, $100 is what you expect in return, AT THE VERY LEAST. Here is the problem. Because of the "need" of intimacy being felt, expectations and satisfaction on the return on the investments are lowered. I overvalued the investment of people because I just wanted to see a return. A return that showed to be low in value. I was so focused on getting love and not considering the quality of it. I considered myself to be an undervalued investment. I could not identify what a person could do for me but what I could do for them. The perspective: if you can show a person a raise in your value, that they will be motivated to match it. Investments are risks and this was the risk that I was willing to take.

Understanding the varying levels of risk was part of shifting my ultimate perspective of love. This is very important to understand. People make time for what they want to in life. Plain and simple. A person WILL make time for what is important to them. We can apply this concept to any situation beyond love and relationships. Think of a time where a person did not make time for you and vice versa. This is something we are all guilty of. But for some reason, we look past it and make excuses thus leaving us more vulnerable in our search for love. We need love and how we go about obtaining it differs. I thought if I gave love, it would one day find its way back. The hard truth is it does not always work like that way. I have made the conscious decision to focus solely on giving genuine love to the right investments and with this, I have been able to decipher the genuineness in what I have received in return.

ANGER

Anger can be a sensitive emotion for a lot of people. It can be difficult to manage and control. Anger allows us to express negative feelings while assisting in finding viable solutions to problems. This perspective on anger is what has allowed me to handle situations in a different manner. For me, it takes a lot to get upset. I am not easily angered or disturbed by situations. When it comes to anger, people often are caught up in the "scenarios" and its supporting casts. People tend to get caught up in the BS. This misguided focus tends to add fuel to the flames, making the situation inextinguishable. When circumstances trigger an angry response, I have learned to shift my focus to assessing the problem and finding a solution. Don't get me wrong, there are times where I get frustrated when I am presented with certain circumstances, just like anyone else. However, I have learned how to manage negative responses and control my aggression by adjusting my perspective.

Instead of being angry with the situation or whoever is involved, I shift my energy and perspective towards acknowledging that I am in this predicament. This allows me to have more control over my emotions by putting a positive spin on the situation, limiting me from dishing out any negative energy towards others. There are too many instances where we waste our precious energy on negative situations making it harder for us to find a solution. This can affect your decision-making in the process and alter your mental state. Yes, it is fine for you to vent about the situation but try not to drag it out. At the end of the day, a situation will not solve itself. Continuous confrontation will leave us in the same spot we have been standing in without any progression.

Confrontation is another problem that is difficult for people to perceive. You must turn a negative into a positive change. It takes at least two people to be in a negative confrontation and sometimes both are not willing to turn the situation positive because they are stuck in their own superficial feelings. If that is the case, be that one person who chooses to turn the situation positive. People may not always follow suit, but you put yourself in a better predicament by not allowing negative energy to penetrate your emotions and influence your core. It is kind of like putting a force field around yourself. It protects your well-being. People push negative energy towards others for one reason: to influence your emotion and to make you feel a certain type of way. Do not allow them to have access to your mind and steal your joy. Be strong.

We are in control of our feelings. If you are angry, take the time to understand why. Certain times call for self-evaluations. There are times where people bring unfavorable circumstances upon themselves. Regardless of what we may believe, there are predicaments that we are in because of the actions we decided to take. I am guilty of this as well. This is where accountability comes into play. You must come from the perspective of "how did I get myself into this?" and "how can I prevent this in the future?" If you cannot address this, you will waste your precious energy being upset with things outside of your control, instead of focusing on what is in your control. For every cause, there is an effect.

Someone once said, "You can't change the people around you, but you can change the people around you." I have no control over what another person does, say, or feel, but I have control over myself. Sometimes circumstances are inevitable, and things happen, but what do you do when you are in that position? How are you going to react? How are you going to overcome the circumstances? These are questions that must be answered if you want to effectively manage your anger. There are times where we won't be able to talk ourselves down from the ledge. We will become angry and at times, lose control. If this happens, be angry at the situation, don't be too hard on yourself. It is important to understand what you could have done differently so you can adjust the next time around. Just like you control your own happiness, you control your own anger. None of this is easy and our responses will not always be perfect. But we try. We must take the time to focus and funnel our anger into a positive light that shines brighter than any star.

PASSION

Passion can influence emotion, especially if you do not have the right frame of reference. Passion is a belief. It is what you believe in so strongly that you are willing to go to the ends of the earth to accomplish and prove. Some people quickly find their passion, they fall in love instantly and live life happily ever after. On the opposite end of the spectrum, there are others that may take a lifetime to figure out what their hearts desire. It is not always easy to find. It takes times to understand what you truly love. In Steve Harvey's book Act Like A Success, Think Like A Success, he talks about finding your gift. Identifying those not so secret talents that God has bestowed upon you. While seeking out my passion, I thought it would be exactly that. My gift. However, that did not seem to be the case. I am good at a whole "lotta" things, but I did not have a single passion for any of them. It frustrated me that I could not identify what it was. From my perspective, I needed to find what I was really good at and that will be my passion, right? Then I realized that I was looking at it the wrong way. I was perceiving my gift and my passion to be the same thing when it's not. I understood that I had to look at the bigger picture of what I wanted to accomplish. Your gift is a part of your passion. Your gift is what you do, and your passion is the reason why you do it. It's your ultimate goal in life.

When I understood this, I understood my passion. My passion is to simply inspire. In whatever I do, inspire those around me in any way I can. I then understood why I do the things I do. The reason I could not point out a single thing I had a passion for was because everything that I was doing was synergistic. Everything was working together for a greater cause. You must understand what your big picture is. Expand your mind and thoughts. Think bigger. Think greater. Then narrow it down. Don't start small, start big. Your passion will support everything underneath and in between. It will be tested and doubted by many and they may not see the vision. If you allow someone to break through passion, it was not your real passion in the first place. It should be so great of an emotion that others around you should take notice.

RED

LOVE - Focus on giving genuine love to the right investments

ANGER - Focus on solutions, not the situation

PASSION – Your gift and passion are not the same thing

Orange: The Color of Comfort & Stability

When you see the color orange, you think of the sun. A calm and relaxing moment while watching the sunset on a nice beautiful evening. It is stimulating and vibrant. When I see orange, I feel warmth. This color represents comfort and stability; two emotions that really taught me how to perceive different aspects in my life. They taught me to understand that the most important things in my life are the ones that I have control over. For some strange reason, we put these emotions in the hands of others when we should be the ones to empower our own lives.

COMFORT

In the past, I barely payed attention to my own comfort level in situations. Your comfort level will tell you exactly how you feel about any and every situation. Comfort puts your emotions at ease. When we are in comfortable circumstances, we feel leveled. The feeling of comfort is our safe haven. Some people make mistakes by becoming too comfortable. Becoming too comfortable makes you vulnerable. You must stay attentive mentally and physically. Comfort is a very tricky emotion because it is one of the few that sometimes you may have little control over. People around you have the ability to influence your comfort level at any time. However, we never have a problem with being comfortable, we have a problem with being uncomfortable. It is a weird, tingling, physical and mental pain. For many, we are afraid to confront this feeling. Sometimes we are scared to acknowledge why we feel that way, so we wait it out until we are removed from that situation and it magically goes away. This is how I perceived it, a negative emotion that will go away.

There was a point in my life where I spent time with a lot of familiar people. People I have been associated with for a long time. I was completely uncomfortable. I'm an introvert. I don't say much. I just kick back, relax, and go with the flow. But at the same time, my mind is running a thousand miles per hour. I had no reason why and it bothered me greatly. At first, I wanted to leave. Just remove myself from the setting so that the feeling would go away. But even then, just knowing that I was uncomfortable in that setting bothered me.

Instead of just making it go away, I decided to mentally tackle the emotion of uncomfortableness head on and transition my perspective. Sometimes it is not the people around you. It's you. You are uncomfortable with yourself. You can be around something different or new. You may even be a different version of yourself searching for acceptance. I viewed being uncomfortable as a bad thing. That it meant something was not right and that it needed to be fixed. So, I did whatever I needed to do until I felt things around me were back to status quo. In a way, I was running away from the feeling of being uncomfortable. As time went on, I was put in numerous situations that exacerbated this feeling. At that point, I mentally challenged myself to finding a way to address it. Uncomfortableness will never go away, but you can confront it.

I started perceiving being uncomfortable as personal growth. That I was transitioning into something different and new. Possibly bigger and better. This helped see me through uncomfortable situations by changing the context from negative to positive. Looking at it from one side of the hill, I did not want anything to do with this feeling. I just wanted it to go away. From the other side, I used it as an experience to further my personal growth, which ultimately has helped me find myself. I mentally grew and matured because these became erudite situations. I now know how to better address this emotion. Don't rush to eliminate this feeling because you feel that it is unfavorable. These nagging feelings can empower you, elevating you to unforeseen heights.

Being uncomfortable plays a big role in improving many aspects in our lives. Imagine being comfortable all the time. Sticking to the same regimen every day because we love comfort. Think about when you are driving to work. You take the same road every day, see the same things, and stop at the same gas station to fuel up. Have you ever driven from Point A to Point B, but don't remember anything in the middle? It's because our comfort level begins to blur things out. We start missing out on things because we have become so familiar with this given path. We must push ourselves past our comfort zone to become comfortable with new things, ideas, and concepts. In other words, we must embrace being uncomfortable.

STABILITY

Stability is not an actual emotion, but the feeling of stability is something that we all experience, and all want. Stability is the sense of security in our lives. We do things to accomplish being stable. Whether it is financially, socially, or physically, you want to have a secure foundation. Many aspects are linked and effect our well-being. Our friends, family, occupation all have influences on our foundation.

I have noticed a trend amongst millennials regarding the perception of stability. Too many times, we examine our stability through the lens of someone else. We look at people that are similar in demographic and find areas of commonality. We analyze what we have and don't have and set out on a mission to "level the playing field." Because of this, we do not have our own sense of stability. Our standards are based off the next person and we fail to realize that not all people come from the same set of circumstances or are cut from the same cloth. We all come from something different and when you feel as if you are falling behind to reaching this stable point, it takes a toll on you mentally. You feel as if you are not doing enough and everything that you have done isn't leading you down the road of success. This entire time, you are trying to reach someone else's goals and because of it, you overly stress yourself out. I learned to set stability according to my standards, based on what I want to accomplish and how I want to do it. Stability can be subjective, so what is stable for one, may not be stable for all. We might be in the same storm, but we all are in different boats. Remember, there are many other factors that influence stability. Whatever it may be, stability is based on your interpretation and not others.

At times, we align our future with our present. I did this a lot. I thought my current circumstances were not favorable in reaching my future goals. I had to ultimately change my perspective to understand that stability and goals are not the same, but it is part of the journey. The goal is to become stable. To eliminate external factors that may threaten our well-being and sense of security. Feelings of instability can trigger other emotions. It is natural. Yet, it is important to define your own level of stability within your own terms and in your own time.

ORANGE

COMFORT – Embrace uncomfortableness

STABILITIY – Define stability according to your own terms

Purple: The Color of Hope

Purple is the color of elegance. It is the product of a combination of red's fierceness and blue's calmness. When we physically see the color purple, it mentally uplifts our spirits. For me, purple inspires hope. While this is not an actual emotion, it is powerful and can influence how you feel.

HOPE

Hope gracefully uplifts our emotions. It puts us in position to take on any obstacle. Sometimes we may feel confident about a situation and other times, a little anxious. But if we have hope, we can conquer any situation regardless of moments of fear. But why depend on hope? Why is it that we "hope" something will occur? I have learned that hope is nothing without action. The word hope kicks in only after we have done all that we could possibly do to obtain desired results. To get to what it is that we need. After this, then, let hope work its course. Don't just "hope" about it, be about it. Yes, maintain a positive attitude. But the cold hard truth is, it's up to you to manifest your desired life, it takes more than just hope.

Life presents us with numerous challenges. Some that we are not always mentally prepared for. I have learned to address challenges head on regardless of difficulty. I refuse to succumb to inaction and let fear or stress paralyze me. Stress is a killer. It is a game changer that can change our lives if not effectively managed. I believe that what is meant to happen, can and will happen. This happens in this thing called life. But we must manage our expectations accordingly to minimize the effects of stress. I had to decide not to allow stress to take its toll on me. After stressful moments, I felt mentally and physically drained. I had to shift my thinking to perceive stress not as that, but as a challenge. When challenges come about, I tell myself that no matter what, I would figure it out. That I would conquer that challenge in front of me and not let it define me. No matter what happens from the start to the finish, I have hope that I will make it through. Nelson Mandela once said, "May your choices reflect your hope, not your fear." Let that driving force conquer the challenge and be that of faith and hope.

Faith and hope have changed my perspective. The faith and hope that I have in God. The belief that I can do all things through him despite the obstacles that may come my way, is priceless. All I had to do was see it a different way. There is always hope in a hopeless situation. A person is never hopeless. Life may appear bleak at times, but it is just that if you decide to never give up.

PURPLE

HOPE - Act upon hope

Blue: The Color of Trust and Loyalty, Sorrow, & Freedom

Blue is a color that represents a variety of things. Blue is electric and friendly. It also can be agonizing. Blue is mainly affiliated with four emotions: trust, loyalty, sorrow, and freedom. These feelings are all encompassing. They are life builders and are the corner stone of our lives.

TRUST AND LOYALTY

The word trust holds weight. It is not a word to be taken lightly or for granted. You see, I trust no one. Not a single person. This is part of my process and part of my truth. Life has had its challenges and some experiences have not been so kind. Trust is not something where you can just switch your perspective. It takes time to build and it takes time to earn. In the court of law, you are innocent until proven guilty. Well, when it comes to giving my trust, you are guilty until proven innocent. My trust is my most prized possession. I am not going to give it unless you have earned it. From the beginning, I must see that you are trustworthy. This is a continual process and only happens over a substantial amount of time. Some people tend to trust too quickly placing them in vulnerable positions. A position where they can only hope for a positive outcome. It's best to get this right from the beginning, because once trust is broken, everything else fails.

Kendrick Lamar, said it best, "All we ask is trust. All we got it us. Loyalty, loyalty, loyalty." You must understand before pledging your loyalty. Some are loyal to no one and emphatically throw the word around in hope of capitalizing on its true power. Loyalty is an empowering emotion. It gives you a feeling of support and allegiance. When you have genuine loyalty, you feel confident. Loyalty needs to be viewed through a glass window, where you can see both sides. On too many occasions, we look at it through a mirror and loyalty is only a mere reflection. One thing that I have observed over the past two years is that loyalty exists at varying degrees. It is relational and situational. A person may show loyalty towards you, but somewhere else, their loyalty is stronger. They have pledged their allegiance to a stronger bond. There is nothing wrong with this until there is. This can become a vulnerable situation where one is willing to do anything for the stronger bond, even by taking advantage of the weaker. We should never wonder where one's loyalty may lie. It should be matched. But as always, be sure that you are loyal to yourself first.

SORROW

Sorrow drains you emotionally, mentally, and physically. It leaves such an empty feeling that nothing can replace what was lost. During moments of sorrow, we search internally for unanswerable questions. Sorrow is emotionally different from sadness. Sorrow is an intense and perilous emotion that blocks out everything else and washes completely over you. It's the emotion where nothing else matters. To be honest, this emotion scares me most. Everything around you is dark and bleak. You exist in a tunnel where there appears to be no way out. It seems as if perspective does not exist in this emotional state. Even though everyone around you has identified one. There is nothing more frustrating than someone telling that the one you love is in a better place, or that they are no longer in pain while your heart is continuously breaking. On some level, you understand this, but your heart refuses to accept it as truth.

But this too shall pass. There is a time to laugh and a time to cry. There is a season for all things. Trouble does not last always. To be transparent, when you are engulfed in the constant grip of sorrow, you don't want to hear this. You want to sulk and live in your misery, but you must fight like hell to escape its grip. You cannot give up and you must finish your race. As hard as it can be to accept, this too shall pass. You just must be willing to allow it to.

The perspective of my own sorrow changed when I realized I must take everything day by day. We get caught up in this emotion because the thoughts of yesterday's past and tomorrow's revised future are constantly running through our head. You are worried about what effect that yesterday's untimely action will have in your future. But you must be present. You must live in the moment, for in that moment is the strength you need to get you through the day. You must also know that everything happens for a reason and it is part of God's ultimate plan for your life. That what you are experiencing is ultimately building a bigger and better version of you and that you must continue to press forward.

FREEDOM

Straight to the point, when it comes to freedom, be free. Be yourself. Be your own person. Do not be who someone else thinks you should be. Be authentically and unapologetically you. Don't be conformed or condemned by someone else's fairy tale version of your life. Their expectations are exactly that. Their expectations. Do not own them as if they are your own. There are instances where we may feel the need succumb to those expectations. Don't. You will never be happy unless you are your genuine self. You have the power to act, to speak, and to think the way you want. Do not live in someone else's shadow. Live your life as you see fit. I have been watched, followed, spied on.... And I almost fell victim to not being myself. I felt mentally locked inside of a cell. That's a story in itself. But I broke out of that state. Being me no matters who is watching and what their agenda is. Steve Jobs once said, "Your time is limited, so don't waste it living someone else's life."

BLUE

TRUST & LOYALTY – Pledge allegiance to yourself first

SORROW - Take everything day by day

FREEDOM – Be authentically you. No matter the situation

Green: The Color of Jealousy

Green represents growth. As a person, I am always looking for mental, physical, and spiritual growth in any way that I can. But there is a complex emotion that can inhibit growth and that is jealousy. Jealousy is an emotion that is ominously represented by green. If you choose to perceive jealously at face value, it will not allow room for growth. But if you view it under a different lens, it will help expand your personal growth time and time again.

JEALOUSY

Is jealousy simply wanting what someone else may have or is it a feeling of inadequacy fed by insecurity? Jealousy, I believe is that feeling of inadequacy. It exists in the realm of feeling that something can be taken away by someone else. For instance, we may be jealous of an upcoming competitor that may take our spot. We are competitive by nature and we never want anyone else to take our position. I don't take jealousy to be envious. This form of jealousy can push you to work harder to eliminate the chance of losing what you cherish most. Jealousy can also stem from a lack of confidence or low self-esteem. It can reflect a lack of trust. Jealousy can portray a desire to have something else that some else has. When a person feels jealous, they are often at war with themselves. The reality is jealousy is not driven by external factors, but from within.

At times, jealously is portrayed in negative light. To be transparent, there are times when I see what others have and say to myself, "Why can't I get that?" I turn that feeling of unease into motivation. I use it as fuel to my fire to get what I want. My life then becomes enveloped in mantras. My theme song quickly becomes "Dedication" by Nipsey Hussle, and I just hear the hook repeatedly playing through my head until I achieve my goal. "Dedication, hard work plus patience. The sum of all my sacrifice, I'm done waitin'." Do not let jealously be the only reason you are motivated, simply use it to get to the next level. Use that little green-eyed monster to your benefit and never let feelings of inadequacy get in your way.

GREEN

JEALOUSY - Do not let it be envious, let it be motivation

Yellow: The Color of Happiness & Deceit

Yellow is the color of sunshine. It is illuminating and uplifting. Like red, it is a color that can represent conflicting emotions and behaviors such as happiness and deceit. These two exist on the opposite end of the spectrum and can generate varying responses. They can take its toll both mentally and physically. They have both taught me valuable lessons over the past two years. Witnessing the reality of the two has allowed me to build myself up mentally.

HAPPINESS

Happiness is fluid. For some, it comes easily and for others, its fleeting and impossible to obtain. Why? Why does it seem that happiness occurs so easily for some and not others? For those that are searching for happiness, it can be likened to a mystical treasure hunt. Constantly looking for that evading pot of gold that regardless of how far you go or how long you search, never appears. You have to ask yourself, what are you truly searching for? How do you even define this thing that has successfully eluded you for so long? We have to understand that happiness comes in many forms and have different angles. One thing that I have learned is happiness comes from perspective. Happiness is perspective. It is the decision to look at the glass as being half full instead of half empty. At some point, you have to be accountable and take control of your own happiness. Be grateful for what you have. Live in and for the moment and prepare to embrace a world of limitless possibilities.

There is a point where the desire for happiness can turn into a self-serving addiction. We want the glass to be all the way full. We become addicted to the feeing. It is that point where you will do anything to sustain or increase our happiness. Let's be clear, a lot of people get true happiness confused with instant gratification. Think about one-night stands, drinking, or even having a couple of extra slices of sweet potato pie. This brings us temporary happiness. A temporary moment of satisfaction. We find ourselves doing things that only mimic genuine happiness. Things that can ultimately devastate our core leaving us vulnerable and destitute.

This addiction can come in all different shapes. We all love the shape and feel of a crispy hundred-dollar bill. We embrace the feel of it and at times, are willing to sacrifice our peace to get it. It is the same feel that we crave with people that we knew were only meant to be place holders in our lives. These people that can only satisfy us for so long. The ones that ultimately destroy our sense of peace because we feel they add some form of superficial value to our life. My view is to be grateful for the things in your life but be willing to cut ties with those things that place limits on your potential. We must carefully identify our true source of happiness. One of my favorite quotes says, "Happiness mainly comes from our own attitude, rather than from external factors." Our own views and perspective are what control our happiness. Ultimately, we decide what makes us happy. We must not place our happiness in the hands of others as we will never achieve that true meaning of gratification.

I once thought that my main source of happiness was success. Of course, anything you accomplish, brings you happiness. You feel a sense of satisfaction when you have reached a specific milestone or achieved a difficult goal. But what happens when this is not enough? I achieved graduating college with two associate and two bachelor degrees in a three-year period, while majority of the time working two jobs. To be satisfied with my life, I completely submersed myself in finding success and conquering my goals. However, I neglected important aspects in my life because I tied success with a false definition of happiness. I found temporary solace in my accomplishments as my true happiness lied in those very moments I neglected. In those moments, I gave others the permission to create my landscape of happiness. I made a mental promise that I would not let anything, or anyone control my standards for being happy and from that point, I have maintained control.

My happiness is not yours and others do not define your happiness. It is ours to find, maintain, and to spread. Happiness are those captured moments. Things in life will not be picture perfect, but it will be worth the picture.

DECEIT

Deceit, deceit, deceit... For a person like me, deceit is by far the hardest to deal with and manage. Deception hurts. It is a weary feeling. A feeling that I despise. Not tooting my own horn, but humbly, I am one of the most genuine people that you will meet. This is probably why it is difficult for me to process. I operate from a standpoint with pure intentions and do you know some people will not even think twice before crossing you. They attempt to capitalize on your genuine demeanor. I am not a naive person. I had some hard knock life lessons, but I am at a point in my life where you can only deceive me if I allow you into a space to do so. Did you get that? If I allow you in my space to do so...My grandmother would quickly say, "Don't be no fool!" Trust and believe, with God as my witness, I won't be.

God gives us discernment. Your skin may start to crawl, or your spirit is a bit unsettled when "that someone" enters your space. God has not given us the spirit of fear, but he has given us the spirit of common sense to quickly close the door on those with ill intent. I will not allow anyone who I have mixed feelings about or barely know deceive me. In order to do so, I have to allow you in my space. You know, close enough where they can tie my shoe. Ladies and gentlemen, that space is sacred. It is your domain that you have ultimate control over. Stop giving away your power and putting yourself in a position to be taken advantage of. Operate wisely.

I am going to throw a curve ball here. As much as discernment is real, so is paranoia. Our primary function is self- preservation and we want to protect ourselves at all cost. At times we go overboard. We are so guarded that we find ourselves blocking those that were sent to be a blessing. You must recognize the signs and interpret given information. In the past two years, I have become exceptionally observant. I notice everything to the most precise detail. I know the bible says, "seek and ye shall find", and if you look at any situation hard enough, you are sure to find something. When we come from a perspective of expecting deceit, in some form, it will rear its ugly little head. Use wisdom. Pray, meditate or whatever it is you do to get into a space where you can trust your judgement. A space where you can identify one's authenticity without risking damage to your core.

Reality check. Some people that you care about the most, will deceive you. It may have not been their intent, but it happens. It is difficult when someone you love has violated your sacred space. This really messes with your mind. It steals our joy. But this is where we start to overcome that mental battle. We have to change our perspective. We have to speak over ourselves and watch the words out of our mouths. No more telling ourselves we allowed this to happen and we should have done something different to change the outcome. No more shouldering someone else's bad deeds. My perspective completely changed. I realized that the bridges that people burn are much more valuable than what they ultimately walk away with. The value that I bring to the table is more authentic and genuine. Adopting this mindset is crucial to your survival. If you don't adapt and shift your perspective, you will allow the situation to control your emotions. You will be angry. You will be sad. You will be upset, and that person will be sitting on their porch enjoying their time because you decided to shoulder the weight of their actions. Doesn't make sense, do it?

When deception arises, move differently. I may not even address the situation with the person. A deceptive person knows what they have done. You don't have to tell them, but your actions should. From your body language to how quickly you shift gears and switch lanes, it should let them know that you do not have time for their trivial nonsense.

YELLOW

HAPPINESS – Do not settle for temporary satisfaction. Control your destiny

DECEIT – Protect your sacred space. Let your response speak volumes

Closing Thoughts

There are times where I thought I would never make it through. Times when I did not understand how or why I felt the way I felt during times of distress. It took a recurring set of experiences for me to gain and shift my perspective. The ability to effectively shift one's perspective can and will change lives. Perspective is everything. It will help choose a path less traveled. Various outcomes and difficult situations can be minimized if we chose to view them differently.

Nipsey Hussle said "They say every man is defined by his reaction to any given situation." I truly believe that. Anytime there is a situation, I put myself in other's people shoes. I think to myself how I would want to be treated if the tables were turned. That influences how I react. I've been called weird, boujee, a "know it all", and plenty of more things behind my back. Things that I know for a fact that people have said about me. But none of those people ever looked at the situation the same way I did. They never looked through the lens of my frames and thought about how I may have perceived it, although I did that for them. I allow my reaction to speak volumes. I allow my reaction to be my persona and define my character.

Some days I feel like I am no different than the next person, yet on others, I completely see myself in a lane of my own. There was a point in my life where I believed that I would never change. I believed that I would constantly be held captive to my own emotions. But God said, "Not So." He placed me on a transformational path that has forever changed my life. When you feel hopeless, when you feel lost, when fear overtakes your core, and it feels all hope is gone, just remember to shift. To view life situations as a precious opportunity that God has given you the tools to overcome. Shift your perspective. Change your life.

In November 2018, I wrote this poem during the midst of this perspective changing journey....

Dear Butterfly,

Thank you for preparing me for this exact moment

The homeless living infused my ambition

The homes that weren't homes taught me solidity

Three-hour early morning bus rides to go to school in an effectual environment trained my efficiency

Mental overburden sharpened my focus

Confusion and uncertainty enlarged my self-belief

Self-reliance enhanced my guidance

Days where I continuously talked but never spoke aloud

and if such a thing called luck had ever existed then I knew the worst of it

Does everything really all happen for a reason?

Every masterpiece has its imperfections

Yet it's still a masterpiece

My beating heart is inspiration

My fearless mind is motivation

I will leave a legacy